# Let's Go Yankees!

## An Unforgettable Trip to the Ballpark

## Scott Pitoniak
### Illustrated by Rob Peters

ASCEND BOOKS
www.ascendbooks.com

Requests for permission should be addressed to: Ascend Books, LLC, Attn: Rights and Permissions Department, 7221 West 79th Street, Suite 206, Overland Park, KS 66204

10 9 8 7 6 5 4 3 2 1

ISBN: print book 978-0-9989224-3-0
ISBN: e-book 978-0-9989224-4-7
Library of Congress Control Number:  2017941643

Publisher: Bob Snodgrass
Editor: Teresa Bruns Sosinski
Publication Coordinator: Molly Gore
Sales and Marketing: Lenny Cohen
Dust Jacket, Book Design, and Illustrations: Rob Peters

The goal of Ascend Books is to publish quality works.  With that goal in mind, we are proud to offer this book to our readers.  Please notify the publisher of any erroneous credits or omissions, and corrections will be made to subsequent editions/future printings.  Please note, however, that the story, experiences, and the words are those of the authors alone.

Printed in Canada

www.ascendbooks.com

# Dedication

Dedicated to my dad, who took me to my first Yankees game at the old stadium in 1966, and to all the loyal Yankee fans, past, present and future.

# Contents

"Hey, you young pups," called Poppy the Dog.
"Come here! I have a present for you!"

"What is it? What is it?" Cammie and Oscar
asked, jumping up and down excitedly.

"Close your eyes and hold out your
paws," Poppy said to his grand-puppies.
"And I will give you your surprise."

Cammie and Oscar did as Poppy asked. When they opened their eyes, they saw a piece of cardboard with numbers, words and a picture of Yankee Stadium in each of their paws.

"What is this, Poppy?" Cammie and Oscar asked.

"These are tickets to a New York Yankees baseball game," he chuckled. "You've heard me tell stories about going to Yankees games with my Grand Poppy and how much fun we had yelling 'Let's Go Yankees!' Well, I'm taking you to your first Yankees game on Saturday."

Cammie and Oscar jumped up and down again. They loved spending time with their grandfather and now they were going to their first Yankees' baseball game. They were so excited, their paws almost touched the ceiling.

"All right, Poppy!" Oscar shouted.

"You're the best!" Cammie exclaimed.

The grand-puppies hugged Poppy, grabbed their baseball gloves and ran outside to play catch. "Let's Go Yankees!" they chanted loudly while throwing the ball back and forth in their backyard.

Poppy was as excited as Cammie and Oscar were. Taking his grand-puppies to their first Yankees game would be so much fun. It would continue a family tradition that began long before Poppy was born.

Poppy wanted Cammie and Oscar to see all the different kinds of animals who were Yankee fans, too. He wanted them to understand that animals come in different shapes, sizes, colors and ages, but despite their differences they could all get along and have lots of fun together cheering for the Yankees.

He wanted them to learn about the game and the many players who had made the Yankees the most successful team in Major League Baseball history.

After playing catch, Cammie and Oscar came inside to rest and have lemonade with Poppy.

"How long have you been a Yankees fan, Poppy?" Cammie asked.

"I've been watching Yankees games since I was a young pup like you," Poppy said. "My grandfather went to his first Yankees game in 1927. He took my dad to his first game in 1947. Then my dad took me to my first game in 1966, and I took your mom and uncle to their first game in 1998."

"Wow!" Oscar exclaimed. "The Yankees have been a part of our family forever."

"Yes, Oscar, they have," Poppy smiled. "And on Saturday, you and your sister will keep that Yankee tradition going. You will see for yourselves how the Yankees have been a part of a lot of different families for a very long time!"

Saturday finally arrived! Poppy held his grand-puppies' paws as they boarded the crowded New York City Subway car for the train ride to Yankee Stadium in the Bronx. Looking around at the different animals, Cammie and Oscar were quiet. Elephants and cats and bears and frogs sat in the seats or stood in the aisle. Giraffes and rabbits and robins and camels and even other dogs were on the subway, too. Almost every animal was wearing a navy blue Yankees baseball cap with white NY letters.

A camel smiled as she looked at Poppy, Cammie and Oscar wearing Yankee ballcaps. "I bet I can guess where you're going," the camel said. "Yankee Stadium! I am, too."

"So are we," said a family of cats and kittens.

"We are going to Yankee Stadium, too," said two tall giraffes.

"Let's Go Yankees!" shouted three rabbits.

Cammie and Oscar smiled. They began chanting "Let's Go Yankees!" too, and soon everyone in the subway car was chanting it.

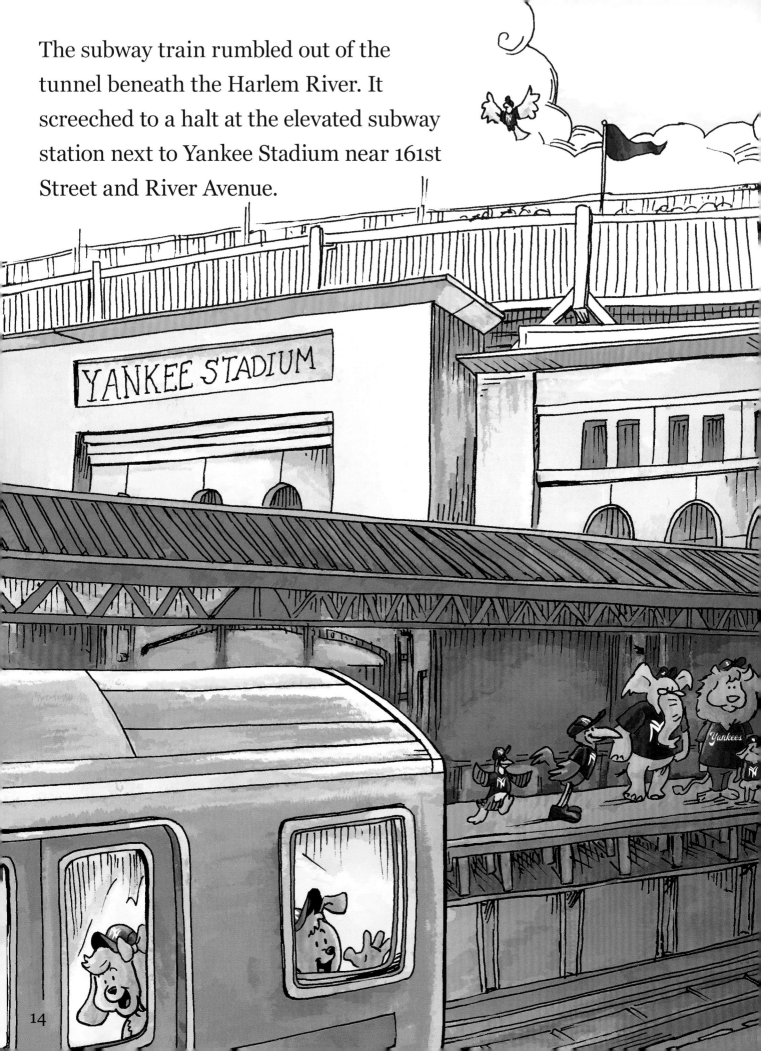

The subway train rumbled out of the tunnel beneath the Harlem River. It screeched to a halt at the elevated subway station next to Yankee Stadium near 161st Street and River Avenue.

Poppy and his grand-puppies left the train and walked
down the stairs toward the nearest stadium gate.
Their tickets were scanned by an usher and they
walked through the turnstiles.

"Let's go to Monument Park here at Yankee Stadium, so you can learn some Yankees' baseball history," Poppy told them.

In the front of Monument Park beyond the centerfield wall, they saw a row of white circles with navy blue pinstripes. Each circle had a different big blue number in the center.

"Poppy, why are all these numbers here?" Cammie asked.

"Players, coaches and managers for the Yankees are given numbers for the backs of their shirts," Poppy explained. "The numbers you see here are from the best players and managers the Yankees have ever had. These numbers are 'retired' and no one who plays for the Yankees can wear these numbers again. It is a way to show respect and admiration for these players and managers."

"The first number the Yankees retired was 4," Poppy continued. "It was Lou Gehrig's number and he was a great first baseman.

"3 was Babe Ruth's number. He was the greatest player of all-time. My grandfather loved watching Gehrig and Ruth play.

18

"And the number 5 was for Joe DiMaggio. He was my dad's favorite player. And 7 was retired in honor of Mickey Mantle. He was Poppy's favorite player. Nobody hit the ball harder or farther than Mickey. He could hit the ball up into the clouds."

"Who wore *44*, Poppy?" Oscar asked.

"That was Reggie Jackson's number," Poppy explained. "He hit three home runs in a single World Series game in 1977!"

Poppy, Cammie and Oscar looked next at the stone monuments and the plaques on the wall in back of the retired numbers.

"This big monument is for George Steinbrenner," Poppy said. "He owned the Yankees longer than anyone ever did. They called him The Boss."

"Now, let's go sit in our seats," Poppy said. "But, first we will buy some peanuts!"

"Yea!" Cammie and Oscar shouted excitedly.

Poppy bought each of them a bag of peanuts and they walked to their seats near right field.

"Wow!" Oscar shouted. "Look at how big this place is! I've never seen any place this huge!"

Cammie pointed to the outfield. "Poppy, look at all the grass out there! I'm glad I don't have to mow that big yard!"

The Yankees were taking batting practice. Some balls were hit into the bleacher seats near them. An elephant reached up with his trunk and caught one ball and then another. He looked at Cammie and Oscar.

"Here, you can have these balls as a souvenir of your first Yankees baseball game," the elephant said. "Take them home and play catch."

"Thank you," Cammie said.

"Thank you," Oscar said.

"This is awesome."

Before the game started, the announcer asked everyone to stand for the national anthem. Poppy told his grand-puppies to remove their baseball caps and hold them over their hearts. They listened to the singing of the *Star-Spangled Banner.*

Before the first pitch was thrown to start the game, a cat in the bleachers got everyone's attention. "All right, Yankee fans," he shouted. "There's a reason our team has won more World Series championships than any team in history. It's because we have great players and loyal fans. Let's do the roll call!"

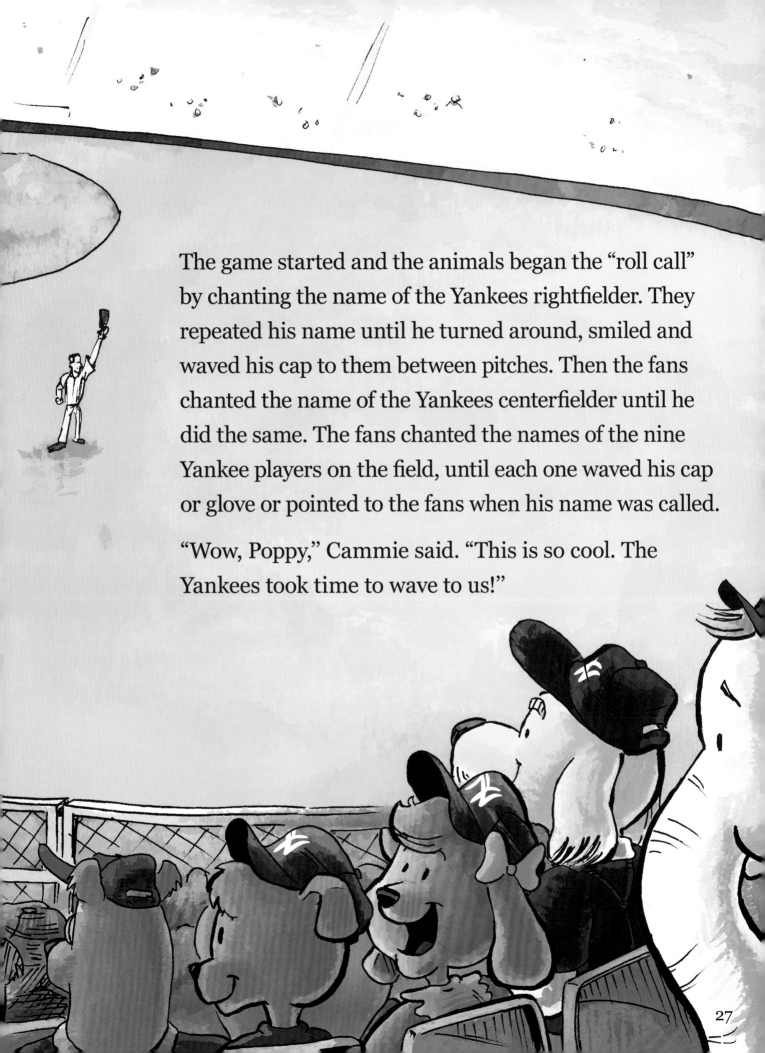

The game started and the animals began the "roll call" by chanting the name of the Yankees rightfielder. They repeated his name until he turned around, smiled and waved his cap to them between pitches. Then the fans chanted the name of the Yankees centerfielder until he did the same. The fans chanted the names of the nine Yankee players on the field, until each one waved his cap or glove or pointed to the fans when his name was called.

"Wow, Poppy," Cammie said. "This is so cool. The Yankees took time to wave to us!"

In the bottom of the first inning, everyone in the stadium clapped their paws, hooves or wings when Derek Jeter came to bat.

"Why is everyone so excited?" Cammie asked.

"Because Derek Jeter is the most popular player on the Yankees team today," Poppy said. "Everybody loves how Derek plays hard all the time. He gives his best every second he's on the field."

"Plus," Poppy continued, "the fans realize something special could happen today. Derek Jeter needs just two hits to have a total of 3,000 hits for his career."

Just then, Jeter hit a single to left field and the fans roared even louder.

"One more to go for 3,000," Cammie told her grandpa.

In the third inning, Jeter came to bat again. All the animals were on their feet.

"Poppy, I can't see," Oscar said.

A bear standing in front of Poppy turned around and asked, "Would you like me to lift your little grand-pup up so he can see?" Poppy and Oscar both said yes and the bear held Oscar high in the air so he could see Derek Jeter bat.

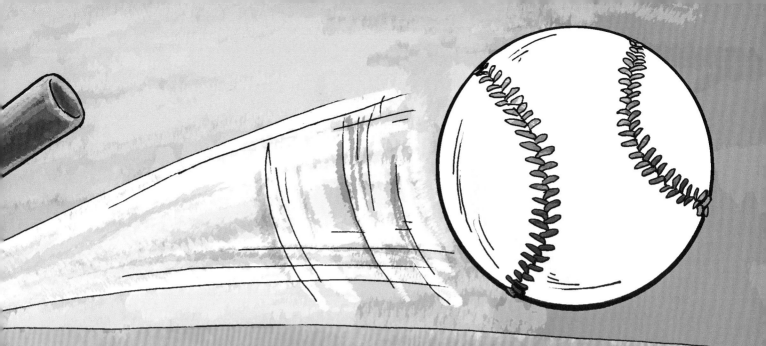

The other team's pitcher threw a pitch. Jeter swung hard and the ball flew high in the air and over the left-field fence for a home run. Everyone cheered and jumped up and down as Jeter trotted around the bases.

"We've just witnessed history," screeched one of the robins sitting nearby. "Base hit number 3,000! Jeter is the 28th player in baseball history to make 3,000 hits!"

After Jeter touched home plate, one of the cats in the bleachers began chanting his name. Soon, everyone in Yankee Stadium was chanting Derek Jeter's name.

The next three times Jeter came to bat, the crowd roared loudly. And each time Jeter got a hit. He finished the day with five hits in five at-bats. In his final at-bat in the eighth inning, Jeter hit a single that drove in the go-ahead run in the Yankees' 5-4 victory.

What a game!

Poppy and the grand-puppies walked out of Yankee Stadium as Frank Sinatra's song, *New York, New York,* played over the loudspeakers.

"Derek Jeter is my favorite player," Oscar said.

"Mine, too," Cammie said. "He's like Mickey Mantle, Babe Ruth and Joe DiMaggio."

"Yes, he is," Poppy said.

Poppy, Cammie, Oscar and the other Yankee fans walked up the stairs to the elevated station and into the subway car that would take them home.

"Poppy, Poppy," Cammie said, "Can we go to another Yankees game sometime?"

Poppy smiled, nodding his head yes. He could see that Cammie and Oscar would be loyal New York Yankee fans, just like him.

"Everyone was so nice today," Oscar said. "Remember the bear who lifted me up so I could see Derek Jeter bat?"

"And remember the elephant who gave us the baseballs?" Cammie said. "Yankee fans are the best! We love the Yankees!"

They looked at all the different animals in the subway car. There were dogs and elephants, frogs and bears, camels and cats, giraffes, robins and rabbits. Everyone was having fun being together. Their love of the New York Yankees made them like a family.

As the subway train rumbled down the tracks, Cammie yelled, "Let's Go Yankees!" and every animal joined in the chant.

Poppy chuckled. A family tradition was continuing. For his family and so many other families.

# All Things Yankees

## Terms, Names, Quotes & Numbers

New York Yankees history is filled with colorful characters, nicknames, quotes, great accomplishments and memorable games. Here is a glossary of important terms, names, quotes and numbers.

**Mel Allen.** The Yankees primary radio and television announcer from 1939 through 1964. His many World Series broadcasts made his voice familiar to fans around the country.

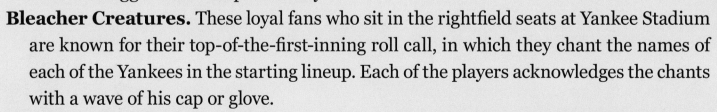

**Babe Ruth.** His real first name was George, but everyone knew him as Babe. Regarded as the greatest player in baseball history, Ruth was purchased from the Boston Red Sox in 1920 for $125,000 and a $350,000 loan. Also called the Bambino and the Sultan of Swat, Ruth batted the Yankees to several World Series titles and made the game popular throughout America with his record-setting home runs and bigger-than-life personality.

**Bleacher Creatures.** These loyal fans who sit in the rightfield seats at Yankee Stadium are known for their top-of-the-first-inning roll call, in which they chant the names of each of the Yankees in the starting lineup. Each of the players acknowledges the chants with a wave of his cap or glove.

**The Boss.** Nickname for demanding, longtime Yankees owner George Steinbrenner. He said owning the Yankees was like owning the *Mona Lisa*, a famous painting. Under Steinbrenner's ownership the team won seven World Series and set several attendance records.

**Bronx Bombers**. That's what sportswriters call the Yankees because their stadium is in the Bronx, a New York City borough, and because of their history hitting many home runs or "bombs."

**The Captains.** In 1912, Hal Chase became the first of 11 Yankees to serve as official team captain. After Lou Gehrig's retirement in 1939, New York went without a captain until Thurman Munson in 1976. The Yankees have not named a captain since Derek Jeter retired after the 2014 season.

**Called Shot.** In the top of the fifth inning of Game 3 of the 1932 World Series at Chicago's Wrigley Field, Babe Ruth pointed toward the centerfield bleachers before hitting a long home run there. To this day, historians and baseball fans debate whether Ruth predicted he was going to hit a home run after pointing.

**Core Four.** Name given to four home-grown Yankee stars who were members of the starting lineup by 1996 – shortstop Derek Jeter, pitcher Andy Pettitte, reliever Mariano Rivera and catcher Jorge Posada. Another player, who preceded the Core Four by a few years but is often mentioned with them, is centerfielder Bernie Williams.

**Billy Crystal.** Many celebrities are Yankee fans, but perhaps none is more passionate than Crystal, the famous comedian/actor/director. He became a fan after attending a game in 1956 in which Mickey Mantle nearly hit a ball out of Yankee Stadium. To celebrate his 60th birthday, the Yankees let Crystal bat during an exhibition game. He fouled a pitch down the rightfield line before striking out.

**Donnie Baseball.** Nickname given to first baseman Don Mattingly, one of the most popular Yankees of all-time. He won a batting title and American League MVP award in the 1980s.

**Elston Howard.** He was the first African-American signed by the Yankees and the first black to win an American League Most Valuable Player Award (1963). After his playing days, he was a respected coach with the Yankees.

*Enter Sandman.* This song by the rock group, Metallica, blared over the loudspeakers whenever relief pitcher Mariano Rivera entered the game. Rivera recorded 652 saves, more than any pitcher in baseball history.

**The façade.** This white, scalloped panel that lines the roof above the third deck of Yankee Stadium is the ballpark's most familiar feature, and is a replica of the façade that was part of the original Yankee Stadium. It's also known as the frieze.

**Female pioneer.** Suzyn Waldman is the first female broadcaster in Yankees history, and one of the first in Major League Baseball history. She has worked Yankee games on television and radio since the 1990s.

**Five-for-five.** The Yankees won five consecutive World Series titles from 1949-1953, a record that hasn't been matched.

**Whitey Ford.** Nicknamed the "Chairman of the Board", Ford remains the winningest pitcher in Yankees history with 236 victories. He also threw 45 shutouts and has a World Series record 10 wins and a Fall Classic 33 1/3 scoreless inning streak.

**From goat to hero.** Two years after giving up a World Series winning home run to Bill Mazeroski, Yankees pitcher Ralph Terry threw a 1-0 shutout in Game Seven to win the 1962 Fall Classic.

**Grand slams.** Lou Gehrig hit 23 home runs with the bases loaded during his Yankees career. That was a baseball record until Yankees third baseman Alex Rodriguez, nicknamed A-Rod, hit his 24th while playing for the Yankees in 2013. A-Rod finished his career with 25.

*God Bless America!* After the terrorist attacks on New York City on September 11, 2001, the Yankees began a patriotic tradition which continues today by playing the song *God Bless America* during the seventh-inning stretch.

**"Going, going, gone!"** Familiar home run call by broadcaster Mel Allen, who also liked to say, "How about that!" whenever a Yankee player did something extraordinary.

**Hall of Famers.** The Yankees have had more players, managers and administrators inducted into the National Baseball Hall of Fame in Cooperstown than any other team.

*Here Come the Yankees.* Official theme song of the Yankees since 1967. It was composed by Bob Bundin and Lou Stallman of Columbia Records and is played at the start and end of all Yankee radio broadcasts.

**Highlanders.** After relocating from Baltimore to New York City in 1903, the Yankees were known as the Highlanders or Hilltoppers because they played at a park at one of the highest points in Manhattan. After moving to the Polo Grounds ballpark 10 years later, they officially became known as the Yankees or Yanks because it was shorter than Highlanders and fit into newspaper headlines better.

**"Holy Cow!"** Favorite phrase of excitable former Yankees shortstop and broadcaster Phil Rizzuto. When they retired Rizzuto's jersey in 1985, his many gifts included a real cow.

**The House That Ruth Built.** Sportswriter Fred Lieb called the original Yankee Stadium this after Babe Ruth hit his first of many home runs there on Opening Day 1923. The nickname stuck. The Stadium, which also became known as the Home of Champions because of all the Yankees World Series victories, housed the team through the 2008 season.

**"Yet today I consider myself the luckiest man on the face of this earth."** These are the most memorable words in Yankees history said by Lou Gehrig on July 4, 1939, at Yankee Stadium. His remarks became known as "the Gettysburg Address of baseball."

**Iron Horse.** Nickname given to Lou Gehrig, who played in 2,130 consecutive games from 1925 until 1939.

**"It Ain't Over 'til It's Over"** One of many popular and funny sayings by Yankees catcher Yogi Berra, who also said, "When you come to a fork in a road, take it," and "It's déjà vu all over again."

**Derek Jeter.** One of the most respected players in baseball history, Jeter finished as the Yankees all-time leader in hits, doubles and games played. His 3,465 hits are most ever by a shortstop and sixth all-time in baseball annals. On May 14, 2017 – Mother's Day – Jeter's No. 2 jersey was retired in a ceremony between games of a doubleheader at Yankee Stadium.

**Jim Dandy.** Pitcher Jim Abbott, who was born without a right hand, provided one of the most inspirational performances in Yankees history on September 4, 1993, when he pitched a no-hitter against the Cleveland Indians.

**Joltin' Joe.** Nickname given to Yankees Hall of Fame centerfielder Joe DiMaggio. The graceful outfielder also was known as the Yankee Clipper after a tall type of sail boat. DiMaggio's greatest achievement occurred during the 1941 season when he got a hit in 56 consecutive games, a record that may never be broken.

**All Rise for the Judge!** In 2017, 6-foot-7, 282-pound Yankees outfielder Aaron Judge hit the longest homer in new Yankee Stadium history and won the All-Star Game Home Run Derby. He also broke Joe DiMaggio's franchise rookie record for homers in a season. In a fun-loving gesture, the team built a replica of a judge's chambers in the right field stands and fans wore wigs and navy blue robes.

**"Let's Go Yankees!"** Favorite chant of Yankee fans. There are moments during big games when it seems like everyone in Yankee Stadium is chanting it together.

**Louisiana Lightning.** Nickname given to Yankees pitcher Ron Guidry, who came from Louisiana and set a team record with 18 strikeouts in a single game and went 25-3 in 1978 when he won the Cy Young Award.

**Jeffrey Maier.** New York won Game 1 of the 1996 American League Championship Series when Maier, a 12-year-old Yankees fan, reached over the rightfield wall and deflected a ball hit by Derek Jeter that was headed for a Baltimore Orioles outfielder's glove. Umpires reviewed the play and instead of ruling it was an out because of fan interference, Jeter was awarded a home run. The Yankees went on to win the game, the series and the World Series.

**M&M Boys.** Nickname given to Yankee sluggers Mickey Mantle and Roger Maris during the 1961 season when they combined for a record 115 home runs – most ever by two teammates in the same season.

**Billy Martin.** Yankee fans loved his intensity as both a player and manager. "I may not have been the greatest Yankee to put on the uniform," he said. "But I was the proudest." The fiery Martin was fired and rehired as Yankee skipper five times.

**Joe McCarthy.** In 17 seasons, McCarthy managed the Yankees to eight pennants and seven World Series titles. He is the Yankees all-time leader in managerial wins with 1,460.

**Monument Park.** Before games, fans like to visit this area beyond the centerfield wall to see the monuments and plaques dedicated to the greatest players, managers and owners in Yankee history. This is also where fans can see the row of retired Yankee numbers.

**Murderers' Row.** This is what the batting order of the 1927 Yankees was called. The lineup was led by Ruth and Gehrig, who combined for 107 home runs and 339 runs batted in, but also featured feared hitters like Tony Lazzeri, Bob Meusel and Earl Combs.

*New York, New York.* After the final out of Yankee home games this song by singer Frank Sinatra is played over the stadium's loudspeakers as fans leave the ballpark.

**Mr. November.** Nickname given to Derek Jeter after he hit a game-winning homer in Game Four of the 2001 World Series – the first official major league game ever played in November.

**Mr. October.** After he clubbed three home runs in a 1977 World Series game, Reggie Jackson was given this nickname.

**Oldtimers' Day.** The first one was held on the final day of the 1947 season, and since then the Yankees have invited back former players, managers and broadcasters to participate in an annual Oldtimers' Day at Yankee Stadium.

**Opening in style.** The Yankees opened their new stadium, across the street from the old one, in 2009 by winning the World Series. Hideki Matsui tied Bobby Richardson's single-game Fall Classic record with six runs batted in and Andy Pettitte became the first pitcher to start and win the clinching game in all three rounds of a single postseason.

**125 wins.** In 1998, the Yankees won 114 games during the regular season and 11 more during the post-season, including a four-game sweep of the San Diego Padres in the World Series. No team has ever won more games in a season.

**Perfection Connection.** Yankees pitcher Don Larsen has a connection with three perfect games. On Oct. 8, 1956, he threw the only no-hitter and perfect game in World Series history, as the Yankees beat the Brooklyn Dodgers, 2-0. Forty-two years later, David Wells, who attended the same San Diego high school as Larsen, threw the second perfect game in Yankees history. And 14 months after that, David Cone threw another perfecto for the Yankees on a day when Larsen tossed the ceremonial first pitch.

**Pine Tar Game.** On July 24, 1983, a ninth-inning, go-ahead home run by George Brett was disallowed by umpires after they determined that the Kansas City Royals slugger had used too much sticky pine tar on his bat. The American League president later overturned the umpires' ruling. The home run was restored. The game was finished on August 18, with the Royals winning, 5-4.

**Pinstripes.** The Yankees wore white uniforms with the navy blue pinstripes for the first time in 1912. Since then the Yankees have worn pinstriped jerseys and pants at every home game. Some people occasionally refer to the team as the "Pinstripes."

**Presidential pitch.** Before Game Three of the 2001 World Series, George W. Bush became the first active president to deliver the ceremonial first pitch in a Fall Classic. He was greeted with chants of "U.S.A.! U.S.A.!" by the Yankee Stadium crowd.

***Pride of the Yankees.*** Name of the movie about the life of Lou Gehrig shown in theaters in 1942. Actor Gary Cooper played Gehrig who had died just the year before. The film received eight Academy Award nominations, and won an Oscar for best film editing.

**Reggie Bars.** Before he signed with the Yankees in 1976, Reggie Jackson boasted that if he played in New York he'd be so famous they'd name a candy bar after him. The season after he hit his three homers in Game 6 of the 1977 World Series, Reggie Bars hit the store shelves. The chocolate-covered candy bars with peanuts and a caramel center were discontinued after four years.

**A record fall.** Mickey Mantle hit a bottom of the ninth home run to beat the St. Louis Cardinals in Game Three of the 1964 World Series and break Babe Ruth's record of 15 Series homers. Mantle hit two more that October, giving him 18, a Fall Classic mark that still stands.

**Retired Numbers.** The Yankees have "retired" the jersey numbers of 22 players and managers, meaning no one who plays or manages the team will ever wear these numbers again. Lou Gehrig was the first to have his number "4" retired in 1939. "8"is the only number retired twice, having been worn at different times by catchers Bill Dickey and Yogi Berra. Mickey Mantle's "7" was retired, but he originally wore "6", which later was retired in honor of Manager Joe Torre. Mariano Rivera was the last Major League Baseball player to wear "42." Major League Baseball retired "42" in honor of Jackie Robinson in 1997. Robinson who played for the Brooklyn Dodgers helped integrate the sport in 1947.

**Ringleader.** No one in baseball history won more World Series rings than Yogi Berra, who played on 10 championship teams with the Yankees.

**"See ya!"** Broadcaster Michael Kay's call after a Yankees home run.

**Scooter.** Nickname given to Phil Rizzuto because he "scooted" after ground balls.

**Sixty-one in '61.** Number of home runs Roger Maris hit during the 1961 season, breaking Ruth's single-season record by one.

**Smarter than your average bear.** Although cartoon creators William Hanna and Joseph Barbera insisted otherwise, it's widely accepted that Yankees catcher Yogi Berra was the inspiration for the popular Yogi Bear cartoon, comic book and movie character.

**Casey Stengel.** The colorful manager guided the Yankees to 10 American League pennants and seven World Series titles in 12 years.

**Tape Measure Home Runs.** The term used to describe long home runs Mickey Mantle hit after he smacked one in 1953 that was "measured" at 565 feet, according to then Yankee public relations director Red Patterson. Two times, Mickey came within inches of becoming the only person to hit a fair ball completely out of Yankee Stadium. The two homers crashed against the façade hanging from the upper deck roof above rightfield.

**Thurman Munson.** Known for his all-out hustle and clutch play, Munson is one of the most beloved Yankees of all-time. In 1976, the Yankees' All-Star catcher was named the team's first captain since Lou Gehrig in 1941.

**Joe Torre.** He managed the Yankees to six American League pennants and four World Series titles, and ranks third in club history with 1,173 wins.

**Triple Crowns.** These refer to players who lead their leagues in home runs, runs batted in and batting average. It's a rare baseball achievement. Gehrig (1934) and Mantle (1956) are the only Yankees to do it.

**The Voice of Yankee Stadium.** For 57 years, the eloquent Bob Sheppard served as the public address announcer at Yankee Stadium.

**The Heart of a Warrior.** That's how team owner George Steinbrenner described intense rightfielder Paul O'Neill, who was considered the heart-and-soul of the Yankee teams that won World Series championships in 1996 and 1998-2000.

**World Series titles.** The Yankees have won more championships than any team in professional sports history. 2009 marked their 27th World Series title!

**"Theeeeeeeeee Yankees Win!"** The familiar line broadcaster John Sterling shouts into the microphone following Yankee victories.

**YMCA.** Before the bottom of the fifth inning, members of the Yankees grounds crew smooth over the infield and dance while the Village People's song *YMCA* is played over the Yankee Stadium loudspeakers.

**Zero Hero.** Allie Reynolds is the only Yankee pitcher to throw two no-hitters – both during the 1952 season.

# Acknowledgements

Telling the story of Poppy taking his grandpups to their first game at Yankee Stadium was so much fun. And it brought back many fond memories of my first Yankees game with my dad on Sept. 17, 1966. I want to thank my dad, my wife, Beth, my granddaughter, Cammie, and our family cat, Oscar, for inspiring this story. I also doff my cap to Bob Snodgrass of Ascend Books for helping me fulfill a life-long dream of writing a children's book after I had published more than 20 books for adults. My thanks to Bob and editor Teresa Sosinski for helping me develop the characters and the plot, and to gifted illustrator Rob Peters for bringing Poppy, Cammie and Oscar to life on the pages of this book. And I'd be remiss if I didn't mention my friend, Marv Levy, the Pro Football Hall of Fame coach and author whose book, "Go Cubs Go!" planted this seed. I'm also grateful to Yankees players, past and present. From Mickey Mantle to Thurman Munson to Derek Jeter to current day slugger Aaron Judge, they've provided so many memorable baseball moments. Lastly, my thanks to the dedicated Yankees fans whose pinstriped passion and chants of "Let's Go Yankees!" have made going to the stadiums in the Bronx so much fun.

# Thanks for sharing our unforgettable trip to the ballpark. Hope you had fun!

## Let's Go Yankees!